WITH TRUST COMES HOPE

WHAT HAPPENS
WHEN A CHILD SO YOUNG TRUST NO ONE

WHAT HAPPENS
WHEN SHE GROWS UP WITH NO VALUES

THERE IS ALWAYS........ HOPE...

VERNA MCKELVIN

Copyright © 2013 by Verna McKelvin

With Trust Comes Hope
What happens when a child so young trust no one
What happens when she grows up with no values
There is always........ Hope...
by Verna McKelvin

Printed in the United States of America

ISBN 9781628392852

All rights reserved solely by the author. The author guarantees all contents are original and do not infringe upon the legal rights of any other person or work. No part of this book may be reproduced in any form without the permission of the author. The views expressed in this book are not necessarily those of the publisher.

Unless otherwise indicated, Bible quotations are taken from the Living New Testament. Copyright © 1967 by Tyndale House Foundation.

www.xulonpress.com

Table of Contents

Dedication V
Introduction VII
Chapter 1 11
Chapter 2 16
Chapter 3 22
Chapter 4 26
Chapter 5 29
Chapter 6 32
Chapter 7 35
Chapter 8 37
Chapter 9 39
Chapter 10 42
Chapter 11 44
Chapter 12 46
Chapter 13 50
Chapter 14 54
Chapter 15 56
Chapter 16 59
Chapter 17 63
Chapter 18 66
Conclusion 69

DEDICATION

This book is dedicated to my husband, Leon, who has supported me through every hobby, business venture and all my crazy adventures and ideas. Without your support I would have not accomplished any one thing that I set out to do. I have stood you up at restaurants, when we planned dinner. I have had you bring dinner for us at the funeral home, so that we could eat together. You have watched me write, then tear up my manuscript, then write again. As well as you have spent hours listening to my pain, hurt and healing of a childhood gone wrong. I love you with everything in me. You have taught me what a real man and husband should be. I never knew that I would actually meet a man that would come into my life, sweep me off my feet and make me feel like I was "somebody". You made me feel as if I could be or do anything and it would be worthwhile. You make me feel very special everyday.

I also want to devote this book to my two sons. These two boys (men now) are my life. My goal as your mom was to give you a better life than what I had. When I look back I see where I failed in some areas. But when I look back at my role models that I had growing up, my hope is that you will feel that in some areas I succeeded. I only hope that you read these pages and know that once you allow yourself to be completely healed from the hurt others caused you, then you can guide others to handle their pain and be healed. Remember, Trust God always, Forgive others, Pray often, Love your family and let Hope restore. I Love you both with my whole heart.

To a very special friend in Christ, Cheryl Johnston, who came into my path at the precise time God led her. Thank you my friend for being obedient to God's call and thank you for believing in my ministry. I remember talking to you the first time and wondering what your inner thoughts were. A sigh of relief escaped me as we met for the first time over lunch and I explained the book and the ministry behind it. God asks us to step out in Faith and walk where He has already made the path and all will go as He planned. Sometimes we need extra encouragement, a gentle push maybe and without your help I may of never had the courage to complete this book.

And the last that is always first, Thank you, God for always watching over me and making sure that I get back on path. When I would come to a cross road or give up and turn away from you and into something that could be devastating or even fatal, you were there always to get me back on path. Your warm loving hand constantly reached down, picked me up and gently guided me. Each time I could hear a whisper of your voice and feel you breath on me when you said, "No, my child! I will not lose you to this. I have plans for your life, I will go before you. The hurt will have meaning, your tears will have purpose and your work is ahead. You cannot fail or grow weary because I have a plan for your life."

WITH TRUST COMES HOPE

Introduction

How does a daughter who has endured so much neglect and pain forgive her abuser? And then how does she share her story in a way that does not dishonor her dad?

And why should she share her story?

These are questions I asked myself when as an adult I was asked to speak publicly of my experiences in hopes of offering encouragement to others going through similar circumstances.

After each of those opportunities, people responded to me – some in sympathy, some because they could relate, and others because they desired their own emotional healing after abuse.

Many asked if I had my story in book form because they wanted to know more and wanted to invite others who were suffering to read my story and receive hope.

So the book you hold in your hand is the result. And I'd like to be the first to say that I don't consider myself a writer. But after numerous requests and much prayer, I felt perhaps now this is the time for my truth to come into the light.

When family secrets come into the light, the door to miracles can open. And despite many years of pain, confusion and self-loathing, I experienced several of those – the ones called forgiveness, freedom and fulfillment.

The purpose of these pages then is not to call attention to myself or to seek pity or to point a finger at broken people…but rather to point any who read to the reason I survived and to honor the Father who made me whole again.

Before I take you on a journey into some dark times in my childhood, I think it's important that you know who Verna McKelvin is today.

First and foremost, I am a follower of Jesus Christ and I do my best to live according to the principles of God's Word in the Holy Bible.

Next, I've been happily married to Leon for 20 years after my first husband was killed in an accident that left me a single mom at age 25 to raise our two children.

Because of my childhood experiences, I was determined my children would have a good life with every opportunity I could provide. I wanted them to always feel loved, safe and protected. Children can be protected as long as they are in our sight, but as you will read throughout this book, things happen beyond our sight. But all things that happen and things that we do are in God's sight. My goal was to break the chain of abuse that had begun when my parents were children.

Now I work in a career that I love because it allows me opportunities to help people when they are grieving the loss of a loved one.

My hope is to encourage others who have been misled, mistreated or who have experienced hopelessness. I want to encourage people to always look beyond their immediate situation.

If we look only on the surface, then we will miss the point. For every situation there is a purpose. That purpose is not always clear at the time, but be assured that it will surface.

Introduction

When I pass someone or meet someone, their eyes have meaning to me. Maybe it's from the pain of younger years or the lack of influence from others. Eyes always tell a story. It is true that eyes are the window to the soul. We can see sorrow, mercy, joy, pain or fear in other's eyes.

Maybe I can relate because of the alone time I spent as a child, sitting on my bed, looking in the mirror at my own eyes and seeing the pain and sorrow deep in my soul. I frequently wondered why no love was to surface or to be shown, but then I was taught it would be a sign of weakness for the world to see.

As you read, I hope that you will see the gift of Mercy given to me...so that I too, could learn and know more about how to give mercy.

Chapter One

Some children enjoy idyllic childhoods in happy homes with loving parents and grandparents. I am not one of those.

Sadly, I've learned through the sharing of my story that it is not an uncommon one. We see evidence of this today in rampant drug and alcohol abuse and other addictive behaviors. Through even a brief study of this dilemma, it becomes obvious that many have turned to these destructive patterns to block the pain of an unhappy childhood, a broken family, or abusive situations.

And so it was in my case.

Children learn what they live, so the saying goes. Here are a few things I was taught to believe as a child.

- Everyone is bad.
- Everyone is out to get you and given a chance, they will lie, steal, hurt you and use you for their own purposes.
- No one can be trusted.
- The world is full of pain, anger and meanness.
- Tears are signs of weakness.
- Love does not exist.
- No one truly cares about you.

Children believe what their parents tell them. Over and over I heard these expressions of general mistrust.

And beginning at a very young age, I began to experience them.

In self-defense, I suppose, an attitude of coldness settled in my young soul. Because I was not allowed to show emotions, I had to harden my heart…to become cold and numb to emotions.

The hardening process began early on in my life.

Even from my youngest days I can remember, it seemed that I had two lives – the one lived in fear when dad was home and drinking and the other when he was away working as a long-distance truck driver. When he was home, I learned to move into "survival mode" to do what I needed to avoid his temper.

When he was away, then life had a sense of normalcy. Whatever normal is…I really wasn't sure.

When he was home, I couldn't do anything right. Everything I said was stupid. I had been told plenty of times that every time I opened my mouth I proved to everyone that I was an idiot.

And God forbid if we showed any signs of weakness. Dad didn't want his children to be "weak"-perhaps because he saw this as a reflection of his own ability to father.

My mother was always the protector. She always sent me outside to play or over to someone else's home. If I cried, she would always try to hush me and dry my tears before dad could see them.

It also became obvious that my father expected me to understand he was the dominant parent. He was not only dominant; he was domineering.

*****

Chapter One

I'll never forget the time he discovered my fear of the dark and became determined to fix my weakness.

One nice sunny day in my eighth year everyone in my family seemed happy. Happiness as we knew it anyway. Our yard was big and there was a lot of space to run, jump and play. But mainly there was just space to stay out of the way. There was a gentle breeze and we played in the dirt with trucks. I didn't do many girlie things. I also spent a lot of time sitting on the porch holding the kitty or in the yard climbing our cherry tree for a sweet snack. That tree was also a good hiding place.

As the afternoon came to a close and friends began to leave, I headed towards the door of the house. Suddenly a car driving much too fast pulled into the yard. When I saw dad get out, I knew the "normal" day was over.

He swung the car door open so harshly that it bounced back, which angered him immediately. He practically fell out of the car, yelling and slurring his words as he staggered toward me. His face was beet red and his bloodshot eyes seemed full of contempt.

I could feel my heart racing and the fear sent heat to my face when he called for me. *Should I run or should I scream? Oh, why hadn't I gone inside earlier? I could have hid hidden in my room or out in the chicken coop. Some where else, anywhere else, would have been better than here.*

But instead I ran to him immediately when he called because instant obedience was something he demanded of us. As he came closer, I could smell the stench of alcohol and sweat. At eight years old, my mind thought, *Be nice to him and maybe we will leave you alone.*

At first I thought my being nice was working. Sometimes as kids we played in the trailer of his truck. He smiled and we walked around his big semi-truck and he stammered "Get up in the truck, I need you to get something for me." I did what he said.

I climbed in thinking everything was going to be OK. But it wasn't. As soon as I was inside, he slammed the doors shut. Next I heard metal clanking as he secured the latch. It was so dark that I couldn't see anything, not even my hand in front of my face.

"Let me out," I cried. "Please, dad, let me out." Tears streamed down my face. I couldn't stop crying. Even though I knew if he saw my tears, his anger would erupt like a volcano, I could not stop. Like flowing hot lava, my heart raced and I choked trying to hold back the fear.

When he ignored my cries, I remember trying to convince myself to feel nothing. I had practiced this numbness for so long. I started singing to block out the overwhelming fear.

After some time, the trailer's interior grew hotter and hotter, even very hot. The dark, still air was stifling. I recalled hearing about people who left their pets in a car with the windows rolled up while they shopped, and I wondered if dad would let me die in the hot truck.

Then suddenly, the engine started. I wasn't sure what that meant. Was he taking me somewhere, so no one would know that a little girl had died in the truck?

But as the forced air grew colder and colder, I realized dad had turned on the Thermo King. Thankfully, the truck was still parked. Now shivering, I thought, *"Maybe this is my own fault. Maybe, if I wasn't afraid of the dark, he wouldn't need to teach me a lesson."*

What kind of screwed up logic is that, you ask? It's the illogical logic of a child who longed to please her father and make him proud. The skewed logic of a little girl who thought meanness was part of every child's normal.

I can't remember if he said anything when he finally let me out. All I remember is feeling hurt and confused. And to this day, I avoid the dark and cold.

Chapter One

I learned very young that animals are good listeners

Chapter Two

As you might have surmised by now, my dad wasn't very nice to me. He drank all the time when he was home. Mom would even stay away to avoid him.

I came in from school one day after taking a fall off my bike and I was crying. My knee was scraped up and I just knew that someone at home would take care of my wounds.

At first, dad seemed very concerned. He was sitting on the kitchen counter. He asked me to roll up my pants leg so he could see my knees. When I saw those bloodshot eyes, I should have known better. I smelled the beer on his breath and just hoped this time it would be different.

After I rolled up my pants leg, he swung one of his legs up onto the counter, rolled his pants leg up and I thought I would throw up at what I saw: raw flesh, blood and what I thought was his knee cap.

Before I could duck, run or vomit, he swung his fist and hit me in the back of the head. I remember his words, "Stop crying! Don't be a sissy. You ain't got near the damage and hurt that I do. I was on a motorcycle and skid into the liquor store on my knees. You have nothing to cry about."

Well, that was that. *So much for a little parental compassion.* As soon as I saw I could get away from him, I ran.

Chapter Two

This time because of his injury, he couldn't chase me. But why did he hate me so?

But why did he hate me so?

*****

I learned at a young age to be quiet and stay still. I reasoned, *if I stay still and don't make any noise, no one will notice me and then nothing bad can happen.*

Our family outings frequently included trips to the local Moose Lodge and the neighborhood bar. These were "family friendly" places for dad to drink and when the Lodge hosted picnics at the lake, you could bet we would be there.

What kid doesn't like picnics and the lake, right?

Well, we learned not to. Because the picnics meant dad could drink and drive a boat, in addition to a car or truck. On one particular day, we attended a club picnic at the lake. Someone had their big boat loaded with people and they were giving rides. I was sitting by myself on the bank of the lake. The boat raced by in front of me and people were laughing and screaming like they were having so much fun.

My dad decided he wanted to take all of us for a ride. He yelled for me to come out and I shook my head no. Hoping that with all the people around maybe he would not force me to. Or maybe someone would stand up for me and tell him not to make me go. But, again I was let down by him and everyone around me. The sun was warm and bright, the clouds were so beautiful and I was happy to stay right there on the shore.

Quickly, his voice changed and in front of everyone, he screamed and called me names. "Get over here and get on this boat, you scaredy-cat!" You see, he hated to look weak and not in control with people around. When I didn't come right away, he became furious.

I rose up very slowly, wondering *Should I run or just do as I was told?*

Sometimes, if you didn't feed into his frenzy, he would get bored with whatever he was demanding you to do and move on.

But I will never forget this awful day.

No one came to my defense. I was hoping that someone would care enough to say, "Don't yell at her. She doesn't have to get on that boat if she doesn't want to."

I did as I was told. The water was beautiful and I hoped it might be fun. But I didn't even have time to get seated before he pushed the throttle full speed ahead. I hit the floor with a loud thud. When I was able to steady myself and get a seat, I realized that I was his entertainment. He laughed and laughed as the boat flew across the water, smacking the waves and bouncing us from side to side and off the seats.

I was so embarrassed and sat without saying a word.

It seemed he actually enjoyed seeing fear in our eyes. I just knew we would all be killed. Can you imagine feeling threatened by the parent who was supposed to be your protector?

That fear rose up in me again, but this time I refused to cry!

Just hold it in and then get away from him, I thought. *When we are back on the shore, I will just disappear.*

That was the day I changed. I just didn't care anymore. I could live or die and realized that possibly no one really cared, not even me. So, I took my first drink at that picnic. Most everyone was drunk anyway and no one even noticed.

On another occasion we were on Lake Michigan, up at my aunt and uncle's house. My dad was very upset with me because I still didn't know how to swim. When dad went fishing very early in the morning, it was safe. He hadn't been drinking long and he was just quiet. So I would go out in the boat with him on his early fishing trips.

Chapter Two

But this time it was a mistake.

As we were out near a platform, he grew more and more irate that I didn't know how to swim. I remember feeling relieved when he told me to get out of the boat and step onto the platform. So I stepped onto the floating dock that everyone used for diving.

It sounds crazy, but I was so afraid of his drunk driving that I would rather be left out there where it was safe. I knew someone eventually would come by and give me a safe ride back to the shore.

So much for my wishful thinking!

When I stepped onto the platform and sat down, he became furious. His face was red with anger and he yelled, "You are a baby and you need to learn to swim. Jump off into the water – NOW!"

But I couldn't. I was too afraid. And that made him even angrier.

"Jump off or be thrown off," he screamed.

I was afraid of the water and afraid of him, but I did not jump. And surprisingly, I didn't cry. I didn't shed even one tear.

He staggered towards me and I knew that if I showed any sign of fear, things would get worse. *Maybe he will stagger and fall in the water. In my mind I could see him topple right over the side and maybe hit his head on the boat and then he would sink to the bottom of the lake. Could I leave him there? Could I really get in the boat and watch him struggle in the water?*

He staggered right toward me and I knew that if I showed any sign of fear, things would get worse.

He shoved me off the platform into the water, far enough out that I couldn't grab onto anything. I struggled while he yelled, "Swim you little baby."

I tried with everything in me to swim, but it was no use. I can still see his red-faced anger and hear his slurred hurtful words.

I remember thinking, *Maybe I won't make it; maybe I will drown. Maybe I knew right this minute, if he fell in the water I know I could leave him there. I could drive the boat all the way back to the shore and not look back.*

To this day I don't know how I got out of that situation. I don't know if I blacked out from exhaustion or if he got bored and pulled me up out of the water. I just don't know.

I only remember that I no longer like my dad; I simply feared him and I think the hatred began that day.

*****

Another time when something caught fire in our basement, dad was really drunk. So drunk, in fact, he was unconscious. Mom couldn't get him up to help, so she sent us hurrying to tell our grandparents, hoping maybe they would come to the rescue.

My mind has forgotten how that situation ended, but I do know this. It was the first time I had defended myself with an emotional state dad had taught me well: *I Don't Care*.

I honestly did not care if we got him up and out or not. I think this is when even more anger and resentment settled into my heart. I just couldn't care anymore.

Fear and confusion were just part of our normal. We never knew what would come next.

Mom really didn't know how to stop him from his craziness and we learned to steel ourselves against it. I wondered sometimes why she never stepped in to set him straight. *Was she afraid of him, too*?

Chapter Two

My early childhood years were spent hiding out, trying to a void his wrath. I was afraid of the dark, afraid of swimming, afraid of boats and too afraid to shed a tear.

Somewhere around the age 5–7

Chapter Three

Despite my dad's addiction to alcohol, he did work and try to provide for our family. He was away on long distance hauls quite a bit, which gave us all some downtime. We could relax and be ourselves when he was away.

One summer, however, he was home and he'd started drinking very early in the morning. That day I was enjoying myself outside, going to friends' homes and playing in the woods.

As I came home in the afternoon, I crossed the creek into our backyard and heard more than his voice. I stopped to listen and realized that he and someone else were drinking on the porch.

Please don't let him see me or hear me. Maybe I should run or just hide somewhere.

A lot of times in this situation I climbed the big cherry tree to just sit and be out of anyone's sight. But this time I went into the chicken coop.

We had a few chickens, not many, and they didn't bother me. It wasn't totally dark because light came through the cracks between the boards. It smelled bad, but I knew I'd be alone and safe once I shut the door. So the smell was nothing compared to the alternative.

Chapter Three

I found a place to sit in the corner of the coop and thought the clucking I heard was just the chickens.

Then the banging noise started. Someone was hitting the outside of the building with something that sounded heavy and dangerous. I ran for the door. The chickens were frantic. Flapping their wings and bouncing around on their spring-loaded legs. The all started squawking and my screaming added to the frenzy.

When I reached the door, I pushed and pushed so hard, trying to get out. Tears were streaming down my face and my arms were giving out from pushing on the door. I knew I shouldn't be crying: I should be braver and stronger than this.

What was holding it closed and what was that awful banging noise? STOP CRYING!!!! Stop the chickens from hitting me and the noise! Why was this happening?

All I could see were the eyes of the chickens and their wings were flailing. The more I hit the door and cried the more the birds grew frantic.

I need to stop crying but I can't. I pushed the door as hard as I could and it gave away. I heard men laughing. Then I looked up to see my dad.

His laughter quickly turned to red-faced anger. He spewed his spit as he yelled "You cry baby!!" He swung to hit me and I took off running as fast as I could. *Where did I get this bravery from? I am running away from him and I have never done that. Just run, don't look back. Keep going!* I went back through the creek behind the house and into the woods. I always felt safer in the woods. It was so quiet and no one could hear me cry. My voice would not irritate any living soul.

I couldn't stop shaking and the tears started again. Only this time the tears made me mad because I didn't want to be weak and cry like a baby. I knew I had to stay in the woods until I could pull myself together and wait until I thought he might pass out, because I had never run from him and I didn't know what he would do.

Was this really how a child's life was supposed to be? When I spent time with cousins or overheard friends at school, they talked about fun times and how much they loved their family. I wondered, *do I love my family? Do they love me? What is love, really? How will I ever know if love really exists?*

Basically, what I knew was fear, physical pain, anger, mistrust and loneliness.

Sadly, as an adult I now think back and I don't remember even one time that anyone in our family showed love to each other–ever. No one hugged and there was very little show of emotion at all. It appeared that love, like tears, was a sign of weakness.

ROMANS CHAPTER 8

VERSE 25–26

25 BUT IF WE MUST KEEP TRUSTING GOD FOR SOMETHING THAT HASN'T HAPPENED YET, IT TEACHES US TO WAIT PATIENTLY AND CONFIDENTLY.

26 AND IN THE SAME WAY — BY OUR FAITH — THE HOLY SPIRIT HELPS US WITH OUR DAILY PROBLEMS AND IN OUR PRAYING. FOR WE DON'T EVEN KNOW WHAT WE SHOULD PRAY FOR, NOR HOW TO PRAY AS WE SHOULD; BUT THE HOLY SPIRIT PRAYS FOR US WITH SUCH FEELING THAT IT CANNOT BE EXPRESSED IN WORDS.

Chapter Four

One thing I knew from the start…crying was unacceptable. I learned to stuff my emotions way down inside somewhere. What I didn't realize was that any positive thoughts I had were being stuffed along with all the bad.

As time went on, I learned that I showed no emotion. It lowered the risk that anyone would want to get to know me. No one ever asked questions about home or why I stayed to myself. In my own mind, that meant that no one cared. The world was just like he always said it would be. No one would ever care about me or want to ever hear my stupid thoughts.

Continuing along this line of logic, if no one cared to know me, then I couldn't ever be hurt by another person.

We were taught that people could not be trusted because their only motive was "to use you to get whatever they wanted." Dad warned, "They will talk about you, stab you in the back and always blame you for the things they did wrong." So his point was to teach us that we should treat people in the way that we knew they would eventually do to us. We should never let our guard down or trust anyone.

Along with these unusual suspicions came the constant criticism of who I was as an individual. I was learning that

Chapter Four

I was not worth much now and was sure that I never would be anything.

Do you recall times when your family sat around the dining table and had casual conversations about local news or events that seemed to matter to most people? What about conversation just asking about each others day?

Our family had some of these times, too. But sadly for me, they weren't happy times. Whenever I would chime in to offer an opinion, suggestion or idea because I wanted to be a part of something it always ended very bad. It seemed that I just wanted someone to care, even for a brief moment.

Dad let me know very quickly how stupid I was at just about every conversation. I heard him say regularly, "Every time you open your mouth, you prove that you are an idiot."

Just don't say anything. No matter how bad you want to be a part of the conversation. Do not let your guard down. Keep your thoughts to yourself!!!

I carried these impressions with me throughout my school years. I never raised my hand, never joined in conversation with my classmates, and never gave my opinion. In my mind, I believed no one cared to hear what I thought anyway.

Actually, I was never sure what people thought of me. Surely, someone must have wondered why I kept to myself. But no one ever asked that I can remember.

And actually, this made my life easier since I had grown to know this one thing: *I didn't need anybody for anything.*

Steeling myself against the need or desire for friends eventually, then it became a source of pride. By age nine, I enjoyed spending days mostly alone. I went where I had to and stayed gone for as long as possible, just to be alone. I didn't want anyone to see me, get close to me or touch me.

And eventually, being alone became easy. And I found solace in thinking: *I don't need anyone for anything. I can survive all by myself.*

With Trust Comes Hope

Age 7–9

CHAPTER FIVE

Imagine feeling fearful all the time. Just take a moment to consider what that constant emotional state can do to a child's mind.

Child psychologists will tell you that a child's greatest need is to feel safe and to have some semblance of stability at home. Children don't thrive in unstable situations.

In our home, we never knew when the next fight would start, when the next explosion would come. When Dad was home, it could happen anytime. We lived that expression, "walking on eggshells."

Our family moved to Plant City in 1970 and at age 10 I attended Burney Elementary and then Simmons Elementary. We lived in Roseland Park and I walked to school every day. This was "safe" time for me – time to think, dream and escape my troubles.

And I was never certain when specific troubles would come.

When I was 11, I came home from school one day to find him sitting at the bar in our Florida room with one of his friends.

He yelled to me, "Stand up straight!"

I sensed he'd have more to say, so I straightened my shoulders and hurried down the hallway to my room to change into play clothes. When I walked out into the hall, the "fist" punch to the middle of my back caught me totally off guard. Unable to breathe, I fell down in the hallway. When I turned to look up over my shoulder, he was standing there with his friend. Grinning down at me, he said, "You deserved that. I told you to stand up straight." You see, he didn't hit me, but his friend did. And that was ok with him.

Soon after that day I stole my first drink from that bar. We were always around people who drank, so I figured: *If it helps, then I need it too.*

This decision was the beginning of a long relationship with alcohol.

At this point in time it seemed that everything was chaotic. I was trying to blend in at school and it seemed that either I was completely invisible to people or kids didn't accept me well.

Now that I am an adult, I look back and I am sure that they wondered what my issue was. When they spoke to me, all I offered were one word answers. There was no conversation.

I could not hold a conversation about activities. Such as dance class, family picnics, church or even family dinner. Besides I knew if I did, I would say something stupid and then they would laugh at me. If anyone got too in depth with conversation, I would move on.

Don't get me wrong, I didn't cower from people. I was taught survival and told how bad people were, at the same time not allowed to show weakness. So as I put distance between myself and people, the wall went up. The walk was not weak, I was self- sufficient and I didn't need anyone to be my friend. I knew that they would never be friends with me anyway.

Most of all, when I would carry myself boldly and not let others close, I knew one thing…this would make my

Chapter Five

dad proud of me. He would be very happy that I did not let anyone take advantage of me. I then could go home and tell him that I had kids trying to talk to me and I wouldn't let them be my friends. He reinforced his training by letting me know that there was no such thing as a "friend."

Well, I was hoping for, "Good girl! That makes me proud!" But all I ever got from him was that I would never have friends anyway. According to him I probably said something stupid in the conversation.

In school, teachers often tell their students to do their work well to make their parents proud. Ha, they didn't know my dad. I know mom would have been more involved and proud, but she was always busy taking care of dad's messes. She was in protection mode when dad was home–always keeping us away from any area he was in and sending us outside or to neighbors if possible. She didn't really have an opportunity to sit and go over schoolwork or anything. I believe if the situation was different, mom could have been supportive and more involved with us.

Chapter Six

About this time I started asking myself some questions like "Is this all there is to life? Do I matter to anyone?

I didn't have any answers. But what I did have was a parent who taught me that laws didn't apply to him and I assumed, therefore not to me.

Picture this: It's two in the morning and I am a 13-year-old at the truck stop with my dad. I am to stay in the truck until dad returns. He returns with a guy and dad tells me that he needs me to count out the pills he just purchased. He told me how many and I thought that I was doing the "right" thing as I counted out the exact number he told me. But I was wrong again. His fist showed up again to let me know that I was supposed to "throw in some extras" and "steal a few."

The lesson I learned that day: *Doing the right thing is always the wrong thing.*

So eventually, I stole pills for him at the next buy. Then I learned to steal a few for my own use as well.

Looking back I know God was trying to guard my thoughts but I was hopeless and saw no future.

All I knew at that time was that I wanted to be alone because I wasn't smart enough to do anything right.

Chapter Six

To be alone, I often went to the movie theater across the street from our neighborhood. It didn't matter what was playing. I just wanted to be alone and invisible. In the theater you couldn't really see people that well.

The movie "A Time To Run" was playing on this particular day. The main character was always running because he intentionally did all the wrong things. He ran so no one would catch him or hurt him ever again. Along the way, someone told this man about God and Jesus, his Son. And he listened...

This was the first time I had ever heard about this "God" and His son Jesus.

During the intermission this man came out and asked if anyone in the audience was tired of running and tired of always doing the wrong thing. Something made me stand up and walk to the front of the theater to join him. I felt like he knew all about my situation, like he had seen my mixed-up family.

He explained how a relationship with Christ could improve my life and I wanted to believe him. Even though I had learned not to trust anyone, I trusted him. I wanted his truth to be true for me.

Emotionally, I felt touched at the core of my soul and that afternoon I experienced new hope that my life would get better.

Unfortunately, I never got connected with a church to learn more.

But that was the beginning of a relationship that could never be broken. I didn't know all there was to know, but Jesus had now been invited into my life and every situation.

Even though things were bad and fear was a huge part of life, God was in control. A God that I didn't know was there and I would discover that learning to live by Faith involves pain. I would know that our feelings cannot control our faith.

He was there to hold my hand. There were many times that I let go and turned my back to give up, to follow my feelings because I was angry about this situation and this God or Jesus would not fix it.

And life went on…

CHAPTER SEVEN

Once I realized that my dad was having me count out the drugs to keep him going, then I began taking them every now and then, too. I figured that it was ok for me to steal their cigarettes. And if I took their cigarettes, why not help myself at dad's bar, too.

If speed and uppers helped him to drive and keep going, then it would help me keep going through any situation. Helping myself to his bar products would numb my pain that was way down inside.

I didn't realize that my life was going to be very different now. I had met Jesus and invited Him into my heart…into my life. The world that I kept hidden from everyone else, now had someone watching every move. I didn't realize it then, but I now had a protector, a provider who walked with me every moment of every day. I only knew His name and that He loved me. But I didn't know that in every situation Jesus Himself would be there.

The bad things did not stop, but He protected and with a gentle hand and (unknown to me) He guided every move. Even though I didn't do the right things and I didn't give a thought to anything but the moment in time, He was there. Doing what I could or taking what I could to dull the pain, this Jesus, whom I didn't really know was always there. I grew to know Him. I knew He protected me and cared about me.

Since they paid little attention to what I did, where I went or who I spent time with, drinking became a habit. I learned how to take the things I needed and learned how to avoid being caught. Once again, being invisible proved to be an advantage.

While most students my age were making the transition from playing with toys to parties and dating, I was hiding out to smoke and take a drink.

Fortunately (or so I thought then) since my only friend also had parents that drank regularly, I now had two liquor cabinets to steal drinks from.

The only difference was that her parents weren't mean to each other or to us, and consequently, their home became my safe haven when dad was in town.

This is when I began staying out all night. We ran through the neighborhood, smoking our cigarettes and thinking we were cool. We were looked at as the trouble in the area. But what I felt like was that I was known as the "throw away" in the neighborhood.

But I finally found where I fit in. They didn't think anything I said was stupid. They welcomed me into their group and I learned that they were outcasts or "throw aways" as I was. We all hung out together and did not discuss our home lives. They didn't care nor did they ever talk about their home lives. We drank, smoked, listened to loud music and were pests to others.

Was this what "real" family was? It was what I thought this Jesus was talking about–people caring about me and loving me for who I am. Not asking questions about anything. No one said I was stupid and I was learning how to care about people and learning how to love people. Most people talk about kids learning bad things by hanging in the street, but I was actually learning how to care about people.

Chapter Eight

The solid foundation was set for my life. I knew not to get too friendly or too close to anyone. But at the same time, I knew I had my group I could turn to. Today, kids are going beyond a group to fit in.

My instincts, instilled by my father, directed me to care only about myself.

At the same time, however, he constantly reminded me how stupid I was. As a result, I knew I was of no value to anyone. I was nothing to him, but I was something to this group of friends. They cared about me, but did I really know how to care about them?

I existed here on this earth, but felt nothing. I simply existed. There was no birthday, anniversary or holiday worth celebrating. Nothing was important enough to look forward to.

Alcohol became my friend as the frequency of my intake increased. With his very own well-stocked bar, I had anything I wanted at my fingertips at any time.

My grandmother was an alcoholic, too. When she came to Florida for a visit, I had my first experience watching someone struggle with the withdrawal. Our job was to help her sober up and it was very scary to witness the process.

I wondered, would this be my dad one day. Worse yet, would it be me? Either way it didn't matter because I didn't care. And if it was dad and I owned my own home, would I take him in? NO! Absolutely not! At that moment in time I knew that my feelings for dad were nonexistent. We were taught in school to respect our elders. But they did not know my dad.

At times I would be angry, look up, and say, "*So where is this Jesus? What are you going to do now? Where is this "Love," the "Comforter," my "Provider"?* Dad is drunk, he is ranting and raving, while his mother is supposed to be sobering up. To stop her from withdrawals, he would give her more to drink. Now there are two people always yelling, swinging at us and being mean to Mom.

Jesus, where are you? You are my only hope and I am feeling like I can't take anymore! Please keep your promise. Show me how to handle this. Bring me comfort and a hope to go on.

I began to talk to Jesus more and more, asking for guidance and strength. When I would look up and talk to Him, the talk always ended in this way, "*I trust You to help me.*"

Chapter Nine

I do remember my 13th birthday.

My mother meant well. She really wanted to make sure I had a nice birthday. She wanted it to be special because I was now a teenager. She decided to throw a party in our home to celebrate.

I was so nervous that I snatched a couple small drinks to calm my nerves. I didn't let friends come to my house because I never knew what dad would do to embarrass me. What I imagined was him, staggering and saying stupid things and slurring his words or even grabbing someone. Dad had a habit of grabbing us (girls) in places that men shouldn't, and I was afraid that he would do that to one of my friends.

If you have never been around a drunk, let me explain about the odor. It's one you will never forget because it stays in your nostrils forever.

Alcoholism is a sickness. Alcoholics don't care what they do or say, and when they have bully in them, guess who they try to intimidate every chance they get?

Thank God on this birthday, my dad passed out before the party and never showed his face while my friends were there...

That was the one and only time I had a birthday party. I was so glad when it was over. Because all I did was worry about what he would do or say to anyone.

Thankfully, everyone was gone when he finally woke up and decided it was time to start round two. But to make matters worse, he had some of his drinking buddies come over to join him at the Florida room bar.

I left as soon as I'd changed out of my party clothes. When I returned later, dad and the one friend still there were red-eyed drunk. I passed by the bar quickly, heading down the hall to my room. He yelled, "Straighten up! Quit walking hunched over!"

I knew from past experience that he or one of his buddies would remind me with a fist if I didn't get out quick. He was calling me and I heard him! Fear set in with each slurred scream and I just ran. Was it courage that made me run, bravery, fear or just my instincts were in survival mode? I ran to my hiding place in the woods. This was a safe place for me, to be hidden from the world. Where no one could find me, hear me or make me feel like I was a burden or an embarrassment to them.

I never wanted another party after that. Not that one would ever be offered again. In fact, on that day I knew one thing...that I never wanted another thing from him. *How could he treat me that way? Why didn't he love me or even show that he cared just a little? I would accept any sign of kindness from him, even if it wasn't genuine.*

You know how the movies and books portray a parent as being protective of their children? From my point of view, those were just fairy tales, just like love stories. I thought, *None of that stuff was true.*

I kept everyone at a distance because like my dad taught me, I thought, *They will use me, take advantage of me and only hurt me.*

I refused to be weak by showing emotion. But this one boy was becoming special to me and finally convinced me it was OK to kiss him. Soon after that, I pushed him away and out by being hard-hearted, mean and non-caring. When I was alone, however, I cried about not being with him because there was something special about him. I will never forget his face, his name and how he made me feel. At that age, people would call it puppy-love, but this was my first experience of love and caring and almost letting my guard down.

Happy Birthday!

Chapter Ten

As a teenager, I guess the world was safe enough, especially if I could keep people at a distance. By this age, my friends were starting to act a little more grown up. They didn't play with toys anymore. I am not sure I ever played with toys much…I only remember a few times.

I was busy staying out of the way and dodging a punch, or worse, dodging the sting of his words. The hatred that he had came from deep within him somewhere. He would hurt with his strikes and his words would slash like a knife.

While kids were making the transition from childhood into adolescence, I was stealing cigarettes, hiding to smoke them and hitting dad's bar to mix myself a few drinks for relaxation. Dad taught me how to mix drinks and I think he might have been proud of how quickly I learned.

What I also was learning through a television program was more about how God created the world. His son, Jesus died for our sins. He spoke of forgiveness, mercy, love, patience and purpose of life. None of these were making too much sense to me. My friend had bought me a Bible, so I started trying to follow along. I tried reading the scriptures, but it was not making any sense to me.

Dad came in when I was watching a church program. This man seemed to know everything and he offered a

Chapter Ten

Bible study through the mail. I knew I could do that and no one would know. I couldn't go to church and tell anyone my deepest thoughts or feelings. I didn't want people to think I was "stupid" or "weak" and mom always told us not to discuss "anything" that went on in our house. It was no one's business how we lived.

When dad saw a few minutes of the program, it happened just as I thought it would. He began to laugh and then mock the preacher. He smacked my forehead and yelled, "You're healed! God is going to heal you from being an idiot!" Then with some foul language he made me turn it off. But I had already gotten the address to take these Bible study lessons through the mail, so it was okay. I sent for them right away.

When my dad was coming off the road, mom instructed me to find somewhere to go and call her in a few days. There were no restrictions or rules about where we stayed or when we were coming home. She must have felt that as long as we weren't home, then we were safe. I usually stayed with my friend that I grew to trust. By the age of 14 we were hanging out on the streets. People in town knew me and I heard all the talk about how I was trouble and would never amount to anything.

I simply didn't care what anyone thought and I didn't want to be anything anyway.

No one really asked about my whereabouts or how long I would be gone. All I knew was that things were better if I just stayed away until dad headed out of town again.

I just needed to make sure I always beat him to the mailbox. I did not know what his reaction would be if he discovered I was taking the Bible study lessons. But I needed to know more. I needed to understand. There had to be more to it.

CHAPTER ELEVEN

That year I met a boy a couple of years older than me who had a motorcycle and I loved riding on that bike with him. He could not understand that I was not going to really like anyone or why I wouldn't allow anyone to like me. He didn't realize that I didn't consider myself worth being liked.

He also lived with few parental rules, so we began to hang out a lot. Most of our peers had to be home at a certain time or they had parents who expected to meet their children's friends to make sure they were in good company. But our parents never asked, or should I say, *they never cared*.

Mine never enforced curfew, never asked where I was going, never cared when or if I'd be home or with whom I was spending time. I never had a pager either, so there was virtually no communication between my parents and me when I was away from home. It seemed that I was away more than I was in the home at times. As time went on, it was safer for me to stay away. So I stayed away as much as possible.

Some kids envied my lifestyle because I answered to no one, but to be honest, it felt kind of sad to me. No one at all cared where I was, what I was up to, or whom I was

Chapter Eleven

with. Mom and dad had their own issues in their own little world. They didn't need or want mine and I knew it.

The guy I was hanging with knew plenty of people with motorcycles and we all hung out at a club in town. There was people playing pool, pinball, fighting and if you were old enough, then you were allowed to go in the back of the club to drink. But, I soon learned who the people were and if you knew the right people, then you didn't have to be a certain age to get back there to drink.

One night there was a big argument at the club. My friend and I were leaving on his bike when the argument followed us outside. A guy asked where his keys were. He looked at me and I ignored him. I didn't see the pool stick in his hand until he swung it. I felt the blow hit both of us from behind. Someone helped me up and I hurried over to join my other friends on their bikes. We headed out to the Sunshine Skyway Bridge, just to get away from it all. That's where we ended up often to party, to drink, and to just hang out. Maybe it was a safe haven for me because no on bothered us out there.

We also used to go to a wooded area known as the Pits. I never hesitated to drink whatever was available, because after all I was worth nothing, so what did it matter. I'd come to believe that no one in this world cared if I lived or died, including myself.

Things would get really crazy at these parties. I look back now and see all the favor and grace that spared my life. So many times I should have been seriously hurt or even raped. I should have overdosed or been in serious trouble with the law.

But I was spared and I didn't know why.

All I knew was that as long as I stayed away from home and didn't cause friction when he was there, this was all that was important.

Chapter Twelve

My motorcycle riding boyfriend and I were getting too close for comfort for me. I knew he was bound to hurt me emotionally or physically. So that summer I decided to go to New Jersey with dad. He went there to haul fruits and vegetables for the summer.

Once we were settled into a hotel in New Jersey our relationship worsened. I knew I had to get out of there and away from my dad. So I called my cousin in Michigan and she talked her mom into allowing me to stay there.

I caught a Greyhound bus and the trip to Detroit ended at two in the morning. Looking for familiar faces of a family in a big city bus station at 2:00 a.m. should have scared me. But it didn't, it was just one more thing I had to do alone.

When my aunt arrived, there were no hugs or warm greeting. No one said, "We are glad to see you!" It was simply a hello and we got in the car.

My aunt and uncle worked during the day, so my cousin and I could run the streets in her neighborhood. We quickly figured out how to cut across her neighborhood and go to a section across the way. You know, the one that good parents told their kids not to go into. Those kids had cigarettes and knew how to have fun. For entertainment, we aggravated people and roamed the streets. We didn't

Chapter Twelve

actually hurt anyone or their property, but apparently we looked like trouble.

One night soon after when we were in bed, I overheard my aunt and uncle talking about how they had to get me out of there before I got my cousin in trouble. I heard them describe me as "no good" and that I "would cause my cousin to make bad decisions."

So, I decided to call another cousin in the next town. She said I could stay at their home, which was out in the country. No neighbors were nearby at all, so there was no way I could get them in trouble.

What she had was horses and I loved them. My cousin and I saddled up in the morning and took off for the day. We got into trouble for staying out all day until late without telling anyone where we were or what we were doing. We didn't do anything wrong, we just rode to the A & W and stayed gone all day. It was wonderful for me. We didn't see anyone, no one could yell at us and we weren't hurting anything. But her parents were certain that I was going to get her in trouble.

The hospitality was short-lived there, too. Same concerns, same conversations basically. They didn't know where my cousin and I went all day, but wherever we went, they were certain I was showing her bad habits.

So, again, I reached out to another cousin. I went this time with an attitude, because no one wanted me at their home.

This aunt and uncle were strict and had rules for their children, which is something I wasn't used to. I managed to obey for a while, but eventually I got these cousins in trouble, too.

A boy in their neighborhood drove a convertible and he agreed to take us to the beach. The cousins were not allowed to go anywhere when their parents weren't home and getting into a car with a boy might as well have brought the death sentence. I tried to make my cousins relax and understand that teens need to have some fun and that we weren't hurting anyone by going to the beach. They seemed to agree, so we jumped in the boy's car and headed out for a good time in the sun.

My cousins put a damper on the fun that day because all they could think about was how much trouble we would be in when we got home. I didn't get it. I didn't understand how we could get into trouble if we weren't hurting anybody or anything. We were not at the house messing things up or in anybody's way. But they just couldn't lighten up the whole day.

Sure enough, they were right. When we got back to their house, my uncle was waiting. I couldn't believe how it was such a big deal to him. At my house, if you were gone all day and out of the way and not making dad mad, then we did a good thing. But my uncle was furious.

I finished out the summer there and my uncle didn't speak to me much. I just didn't get it, because in the world I came from, we did what we wanted to do. In fact, the more I could stay away from the house, the better. Or should I say the safer I would be.

Looking back now, that was actually a great summer. I learned about how others lived and I allowed myself to enjoy people. I actually smiled and let people get close to me. My cousins had no clue about my home life. I am sure they assumed it was just like theirs. But as you know by now, it was far from it.

I changed that summer after leaving Michigan. I was a different person – one who knew now that even my aunts and uncles thought I was no good. Sadly, this simply proved what my father had always tried to tell us: "No one will care. Even your family will talk about you. People will smile and pretend to be there for you, just to get their own way."

Chapter Twelve

It was true, even though it was a good time. My cousins said they loved it that I came. I didn't know if they really meant it. I just didn't know whom I could trust.

Chapter Thirteen

My dad was actually loved by a lot of people because he could be such a jokester. Everyone enjoyed his sense of humor.

But it was the hours after the visitors left or we returned home, that he would change. So we kids spent a lot of time either in our rooms, outside, or at someone else's home. I would usually choose to be alone – away from home, alone. I would go to the woods, walk down by the creek or just spend time in the backyard. It was simply easier to be alone. Alone was safe because no one could hurt me. No one could see any scars that I knew were on the inside. No emotion. No one could look at me and tell me that I was weak or stupid.

Off and on I was reading the Bible a friend had given me. What I felt was that I was living two lives in the same world. My training told me "no emotion". The Bible spoke of loving one another.

Some days, I would sense there was hope. Other days, I didn't care about anything or anyone, including and especially myself.

As things seemed to get worse, I would spiral down with my feelings of hope being crushed. Drinking became

Chapter Thirteen

---

easier as time went on, I didn't know it then, but eventually I would give up on myself.

Things seemed to be getting worse and I saw nothing really to look forward to. Now as I read in the scripture, I understand. Romans 8:24 says: For in hope we were saved. But hope which is seen is not truly hope. For how can one hope for what he already sees?"

When I read this today, I understand that I had hope for things to be better. Even though I saw no possible way for things to ever get better, hope was still there. Because how can I hope for something that already exists?

So many things make sense to me now. As I continue to tell the story of how things evolve even more, remember: I am not disappointed with all that happened. Sure, it could have been better and I could have had that perfect family and upbringing. But all these things that went on in my life have made me who I am today.

I could almost say that God saw "extra" favor for me because He gave me the strength and the knowledge to continue to press on. But it wasn't "extra" favor for me, because His love and guidance is offered to everyone. We have to humble ourselves as a fragile, small child and allow Him to take control. Letting someone else control our lives and trusting someone (that you cannot see) is not easy. But my friend, I know that God was knocking and I was fragile enough to let Him in.

There are so many times and situations not referenced in this book and I honestly cannot see how I survived them all. But by the Grace of God…

*****

While growing up I spent a lot of time alone and realized that my only friends were animals. I enjoyed spending time with my cats because they were always glad to see me, no matter what was going on. I loved to sit with them and found I could tell them anything and everything and they did not judge or criticize.

Between all the fights and ongoing craziness, I clung to my cat or dog. Maybe that is one way I learned a little more about loving someone.

I loved, loved, loved horses and finally I owned one and spent hours outside with it. I don't remember riding, but I spent a lot of time brushing, talking and crying.

Then one day the worst thing happened.

It was one of those days when Dad had been drinking ALL DAY and I knew by this age to stay as far away as possible. I thought I was doing that pretty well, but then I heard him and his buddies out where the horse was. They were giving him beer and laughing.

Suddenly, the stall door flew open and the men took a whip or something and chased my horse out of the stall.

I remember watching him run through the open field and I called and called after him. But I never saw my horse again. As I called for him, I turned to see them all watching me and laughing.

I hated my father that day.

To this day, I don't know what happened to that horse. All I know is that dad took the only thing I cared about and destroyed my trust.

ROMANS 8

VERSE 28

28 AND WE KNOW THAT ALL THAT HAPPENS TO US IS WORKING FOR THE GOOD IF WE LOVE GOD AND ARE FITTING INTO HIS PLANS

Chapter Fourteen

We moved frequently, so growing up and having the same school friends didn't happen. The most memorable place we moved to was in a community well known as a cult.

I was young and didn't understand much about it, but I knew we were supposed to be careful of the old men with the long hair and long beards. They watched me anytime I walked through the community.

I found a trail that led to a small path and down a hill to a section where there were pony rides, a gift store, an ice cream shop and a pavilion. It was a place I could go where I could be alone and think, or just stay away to be out of sight.

But soon, one of the old men with a long beard and long hair followed me and watched. These men were very scary and some of the things that took place at the pavilion were strange. The men would follow and never say a word. Then when they saw an opportunity, they would speak to you.

One of the men who used to run the pony rides offered to teach me to ride. I was so excited because I just loved being around horses. It wasn't long before he began to make suggestions that made me feel uncomfortable.

Chapter Fourteen

Then during the riding lesson he would actually say he needed to check my seating position in the saddle to make sure I was riding correctly. Of course, he was just making things up so he could put his hands in places I knew they didn't belong.

I went back to this place a couple of years ago. It was the first time I had visited back home in over thirty years. I walked the same path I used to take to get down to the ponies. Not much has changed. There is a book about this community now about the cult that lives there and their history, traditions, and beliefs.

Thankfully, we only lived there about a year.

Chapter Fifteen

At age 13, I attended Marshall Junior High School in Plant City. Here I met a boy I really liked, Louie Rodriguez, and we became "an item". Teens described their romantic relationships as "going steady" in those days.

Louie's dad had a stroke during this time and then another and still another. It was a very sad time for us and we spent hours each day at the hospital just to sit with his dad. I had never known anyone that sick and when he died, it hurt us both deeply. It also seemed to bring us closer as a couple.

When we were at Tomlin Junior High School, sometime around my 15th birthday, Louie gave me a promise ring and vowed he would marry me one day.

Louie added to that vow by presenting me with an engagement ring when I was 16 years old and at Plant City High School. Our plan was to tie the knot after my graduation in 1978, which we did. I graduated on a Friday and we married the next day. No big wedding…just my parents and a couple of witnesses. But we were so excited to begin the life we had dreamed about since I was 13.

Our first son was born in 1979. Louie was a proud father who worked many hours and volunteered as Chief at a local fire department. Through his efforts, the volunteers

Chapter Fifteen

raised enough money to purchase the first "jaws of life" tool used when auto crash victims were trapped in their vehicles and in need of emergency rescue.

Our second son was born in 1981 and we bought our first home. Life was moving ahead, just as we had planned.

In 1985, we took the boys and my mom on a wonderful two-week vacation in the Tennessee mountains to celebrate our seventh wedding anniversary. When the homesickness set in, we headed back to Plant City and our careers. I worked in Tampa and Louie had his job at the steel plant.

On my drive into work on that first Monday back, the radio newscasters described a "terrible accident" in Plant City. I remember a knot in my stomach as I thought, "Could it be Louie?" But then I told myself, "You're late. Keep heading to work."

Before I got out of the car at my job, the radio announcer reported that the accident had resulted in a fatality. I shook my head to deny that it might be my husband and went inside to show the great vacation photos to co-workers.

As I settled in at work and tried to get back into the groove of things, I looked up to see my father.

"What's going on?" I asked.

My supervisor was with dad and he walked us to the conference room. There stood my mother and two other close friends. As they were telling me Louie had been in an accident, I demanded for them to take me to him. I wanted to know which hospital he'd been taken to.

But Louie wasn't at the hospital. He had been killed instantly in the accident I had heard announced on the radio.

*****

Life changed instantly that day. You see, he had been my dearest friend since those days in middle school. And his three-year-old and five-year-old boys adored him.

How does a young family recuperate from a tragedy like this?

As I learned, it was one step at a time, one day at a time, one prayer at a time.

I still remember a fire chief coming to our home to tell me that a car and driver would be at my disposal for five days while I tried to tend to the necessary details of funeral arrangements, purchasing of cemetery property and explaining to my little boys that their daddy would never come home again.

Things were hard....really hard, for quite a while. I learned firsthand the different stages of grief. I wasn't sure how long it would take me to get through and over the anger part.

Louie was killed in a motorcycle accident and his bike was not damaged at all. But when the anger got the better of me one day, I had nowhere else to direct it. On one of those many sleepless nights, I decided to tear every wire off that bike, break the mirrors and knock it over. Nothing I could do lessened my pain.

I was thankful the year that the Hillsborough County Fire Department called to invite me to receive a plaque in Louie's honor as their "Firefighter of the Year." It was a poignant, sad moment, but I was so proud of him and the work he loved.

After the death of my husband, I started breaking and training horses. I have spent hours on a trail and talking to the horses. Poor animals–had to hear it all.

I searched for something that would be happy to see me and for something that I would be happy to see as well. Needless to say, I still am partial to animals.

Chapter Sixteen

A few years after functioning in survival mode since Louie's death, I met a great man and remarried. Leon fell in love with my boys and with me.

I had always felt God had blessed me with my marriage to Louie, the man who was always there for me. Then, when God sent Leon into my life, I felt doubly blessed. We fit together easily as a family and life was beginning to have some normalcy again. Leon volunteered to coach Little League baseball and then he coached football. Life became busy again and we were very happy.

My desire was to stay home to raise my boys and Leon was all for that idea. I met an elderly gentleman who was involved with horses and rode in the cavalry. He taught me a whole lot about horses and their behavior. I decided that I could earn an income from boarding horses and competitive barrel racing. Eventually I trained horses and even broke some wild ones, offered riding lessons, and raised goats.

Being able to spend so much time with the animals (and the people who loved them) and be outside most of the time was good therapy for me. Animals are great listeners and they don't break your confidence either. They can be trusted.

Sadly, we experienced tragedy in Leon's family within a few years of our marriage. His mother called one day to tell us that his sister and 15-year-old niece were both in the hospital iron lung machines and that his six-year-old nephew had died. Apparently in the middle of the night someone had come into their home and set it on fire. His niece ran through the fire to save her little brother and mother. When the firefighters arrived, they discovered Leon's niece and sister unconscious near the back door. After a few weeks, doctors determined it would be best to take them off the machines and allow them to die. So instead of one funeral, we planned for all three funerals to take place on the same day.

Not too long after this sadness, sometime between March 2nd and March 5th in 1990, my 50-year-old mother suffered a stroke and a man found her laying in a parking lot uptown. My Dad picked her up when the man called, but he didn't seem too concerned. Dad had been drinking, so he just took her home and put her to bed. Then he called me and said, "Something is wrong with your mom. You may want to come and get her."

I could tell as soon as I saw her that something wasn't right. She didn't want to go to the hospital, so I told her we were going shopping because she needed to get away from dad's yelling. Instead, I took her to the emergency room, where doctors told us she'd had a stroke and might live another 72 hours. I stayed in ICU with her as much as they would allow and even slept in the hallway when I couldn't be in the room.

Dad only came for a short visit because you can't drink alcoholic beverages in the hospital.

One night I remember leaving the hospital to go home for a rest. I don't know if I've ever prayed so hard before or since. I begged God, "Please don't take her now. I am not done with her here yet." At the time, I didn't know why

Chapter Sixteen

I had prayed about not being done with her yet. But I was trusting in God and praying He would save her.

As I continued to plead with Him, I promised, "Oh God, if you will give me just a little more time with her, I can accomplish what I need to do and I promise to quit smoking, if you grant just a little more time."

This was a big promise. I had been smoking since I was 13 and had never wanted to quit when others asked about it. But the day I made that promise, life changed again. God was working with me and He was guiding me to not only take care of my mom, but also to lead her into a relationship with Christ.

Prior to this time, my mother had never spoken of God or expressed any spiritual thoughts.

I picked up mom every day to take her to therapy. I would sit and wait so I could make sure that she got home. I would always try to talk her into coming home with me instead of going straight back to her house. I worried a lot about how she was treated and what was happening behind those closed doors. She struggled with her balance and she limped. Her mind wasn't as sharp as it once had been and often times she had to stop to think things over carefully to make sense of them. Because of the stroke she couldn't stand very long. Dad still expected her to keep up with the housework duties. However, making the bed was the hardest task for her to accomplish and she had to do it on her knees. I found that out one day when I went to pick her up for therapy. I heard him yelling and telling her that she was not that stupid and she wasn't an invalid so she needed to just get it done.

One day I walked in on a heated argument. Dad was drunk and yelling down the hallway and mom was in her room, crying. When she finally came out of the bedroom she saw dad was standing there with scissors, cutting up her driver's license. He began to throw the pieces at her, telling her that she would never drive again and that she was useless. I saw hope leave her face. I knew that she had hoped to get well enough to drive again. But dad had a way of crushing anyone's spirit of hope.

I started taking Mom to church every time the doors were open. She no longer feared what my dad would say or do and she wanted to go to church. On Mother's Day in 1991, the pastor offered an altar call. The preacher asked if anyone would like to know Jesus as their Savior and my mom wanted to go forward. I cried and felt so happy that she wanted a relationship with the same Jesus I had come to know.

Graciously, God gave us more time together. In June of 1991 I even kept my promise to God and quite smoking. I was able to care for mom and help her through therapy before she suffered another massive stroke at home in July of '91. That day I went to pick her up as usual and found her still in bed. The air conditioning had not been turned on and it was very hot in her room.

I was hysterical.

One day, though, we will finally look at each other again and know that God was part of our lives. I am very, very grateful for God–that He had given us the opportunity to be together, to learn about Him and His Son together. I know Mom is with Him and that all the suffering here is over. She is now safe and happy and in a beautiful place.

Chapter Seventeen

After mom died, I took several phone calls from dad. Every time he was asking for money. When I questioned the need, he would claim the money was to pay this bill or that. For a few times, it worked.

Then I started questioning his problem with the bills. You see, when Mom died I went to their house and sat with him to work out his bills. Insurance provided more than enough to pay everything off, including the mortgage on the house. So I didn't understand the issue with bills.

When I questioned too much and started refusing to give him cash, he switched to "I'm hungry and have no food."

Trusting him, I gave him money to eat. Then he needed money for gas to get to the doctor's office. Finally, I decided enough was enough and asked him to meet me at the gas station near his house.

"Pull up to the fuel tank, so I can put gas in your car." I said.

Needless to say, dad was furious because that was definitely not what he had planned.

But I was determined to not give him any more cash.

His new wife called me a few times when she was drunk. She screamed at me, saying that mom tore up our family. She cussed and called mom names, while telling me how terrible mom was to dad and us kids. She said that is why we were so messed up.

Eventually dad didn't call at all and his new wife stopped, too. I was grateful and wanted to just forget I ever knew him and wanted him to forget he ever knew me.

A few more times he called after that. He wanted help again after he eventually lost the house and was sleeping in his pickup truck. Once, he was sleeping in his truck at a park and another time he was sleeping on someone's front porch. I offered him a place to live, but explained his wife would have to go to her relative's house. There was no way I wanted her staying at my home.

For several years I was sure I would never have to deal with him again. One day, while talking to a police officer friend of mine in my office at work, we discussed our families. I shared a little of my background and explained that if I received a phone call that my dad had died, I knew I would feel nothing. I hated that feeling because I knew it wasn't right, but I was being honest.

Several weeks later, a call came and I learned that dad was very sick. The diagnosis was throat cancer and surgery was necessary. I waited at the hospital during the procedure. A tracheotomy was required and his vocal chords were removed. My dad was never able to speak again.

During his hospital stay, a nurse asked if his wife would be capable of caring for him if he went home. I told her no, but they were determined to send him with her and he would not come with me. As he was preparing to leave the hospital, he pointed at his duffle bag in the room's little closet. So, I got it out, unzipped the bag and set it beside him. Before I could turn back around, my dad had tipped up a bottle of skin bracer and tried to guzzle down every drop. He was desperate for alcohol.

I was disgusted and embarrassed. I was also glad he wasn't coming home with me, because I did not want to

Chapter Seventeen

---

deal with him and his craziness. Shortly after that time, I received another call that he was back in the hospital. It was decided that he should be in a nursing home because his wife couldn't care for him properly.

I went to the nursing home and was even nice to his wife. He seemed to be getting worse. He wouldn't eat much and would try very hard to talk and make himself understood.

Soon he started asking me to come and visit every day, so I did. I would feed him soup and milkshakes and such. He could only eat liquids and even that became difficult after a while.

Then God decided He would have this situation come to life for me so I would understand the meaning and sense the purpose of it all. I learned to read dad's lips and he told me that his feet were dry and that they hurt. As I looked into his eyes while rubbing lotion onto his feet, my anger and hatred went completely away. God gave me the opportunity to humble myself, to forgive my dad, and even to wash his feet.

That was the first time that I had known my dad sober. Thankfully, I could "hear" his voice in his lips the first time he told me he loved me.

I actually liked him at that moment.

Dad had a terrible time up until his death. He was in severe pain and continually looked in the right corner of the room behind him. When he saw whatever it was in the corner, he would scream (a silent scream) and the fear in his eyes was a sight I will never forget.

To this day I don't know what he was looking at, but I know he was afraid. His silent scream was horrible to watch because there was nothing I could do to help. I prayed and brought in a preacher to pray with him and for him.

Chapter Eighteen

Before dad got sick and as my youngest son graduated in 1999, my body was struggling from the pain of injuries I had incurred while handling horses. I think I was also exhausted.

I had a private moment with God and asked Him to put me in a position to help people, even if it was as a volunteer somewhere. He answered that prayer with the perfect job.

You should have seen my husband's face when I told him I had accepted a job as a receptionist at a funeral home. In fact, I can still hear his questions: "You are going to work where? To do what?" He couldn't believe that I'd said yes to the offer.

Since that time when I began as receptionist, I have been promoted to positions of detail clerk, then family service counselor, and then office manager. In 2006, became the location manager.

My work at the funeral home has been the most rewarding work and time of my life to date. After assuming the position of manager, the corporation's marketing director asked if I thought I could open a care facility. So I went to work educating myself on what that would involve and learned to plan for a major construction project.

Chapter Eighteen

Today we still operates a Care Center, adjacent to the funeral home, where we now also do preparations and embalming for five locations.

Because of my own experience with so many family funerals, I felt like maybe I could offer some help to people. Imagine a place and a position to "love" and "care" for people. This was something totally opposite of what I was taught as a child.

It is my hope that with each family we serve, I am able to show them the kindness and care I had never known with my birth family. That is why I say God has taken a personal interest in me throughout all of my experiences.

He has taken someone that felt unlovable, untouchable and very insecure and given me Hope. He gave the kind of hope that takes "trust". The "trust" enough to know that way deep in my soul God would never leave me. No matter what situation I faced, I knew one thing was a definite... *No one could take God away from me.* They could hurt me emotionally and physically, but my God had me covered spiritually.

While working at the funeral home I would make sure I went to the Hospice House every day to sit with dad. I made a promise to visit him every day after work. All the promises that he had broken and the times he was so mean, somehow no longer mattered. It was all gone. The scars were healed and my heart had become softened so that I could be the one to take care of him until his last breath.

I have been down many avenues and roads, through many different paths and have succeeded. As long as I trust God and follow Him, I'm now convinced that everything will work out as He has planned.

So when you feel that you cannot take another day and that there is no more hope, simply trust. I encourage you that when you have one of those days when all seems lost, simply look up. Be *fragile* and ask Him to lead you, to guide you because you cannot see the path to take. Because, remember, there is always hope. There is a "Hope" of a better time and better things to come, that you cannot yet see. But you must choose to make the difficult, but wise decision to "Trust."

Because—*"With Trust Comes Hope."*

Conclusion

Follow the path that God leads you down. If you listen closely for His voice, He will guide you down paths you never could have imagined. When God leads you, things will go well. People may tell you and your instincts may tell you that there is no way you have the skill or qualifications to do what He is leading you to do. Trust Him for He is in control and He will make a way.

You see, I am in a position now that is way above my qualifications. This position is way beyond what I thought I was able to do. But when He walks the path before you and there's that passion burning in your soul, then follow Him. Even if you know there is no way humanly possible, but you know God is directing the situation, then run towards Him and don't walk. Don't miss His invitation to do the impossible.

When I was a kid (and wasn't rebelling) and I followed the path, I became the only high school graduate in our family. Then I took His path again and again to become a vet technician, to break horses, to barrel race, to raise goats and now to manage a funeral home.

I came to this position and didn't have a clue, but I trusted that I would be able to help someone in some capacity. Fortunately, this company has been sensitive to the direction of my path and has given me every opportunity to serve families in very meaningful ways. At the same time I have been able to volunteer and serve a community, even though when I was a kid, people saw no hope for me.

Now I can sit on committee boards, help with community functions, serve this city and truly feel like I am part of something. And to this company I will forever be grateful.

This company made an investment in someone they didn't fully know. When I see people and look in their eyes, I recognize the pain. Sometimes I can feel their hopelessness and I want to make sure they know somebody here truly cares about them. We want to make sure we do everything in our power to help.

If this book helps even one person to heal and gives them hope, then I will feel a measure of success along one more path for which I've never considered myself qualified.

But God knows better...

www.ingramcontent.com/pod-product-compliance
Lightning Source LLC
LaVergne TN
LVHW022000060526
838201LV00048B/1645